WILMA
MANKILLER

CHIEF OF THE CHEROKEE NATION

SPECIAL LIVES IN HISTORY THAT BECOME

Signature LIVES

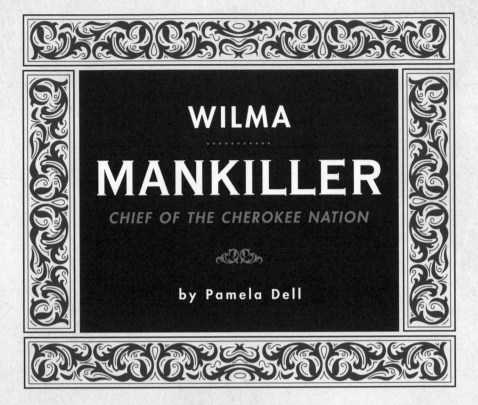

WILMA
MANKILLER
CHIEF OF THE CHEROKEE NATION

by Pamela Dell

Content Adviser: Circe Sturm, Ph.D., Associate Professor,
Departments of Anthropology and Native American Studies,
University of Oklahoma

Reading Adviser: Susan Kesselring, M.A.,
Literacy Educator, Rosemount—Apple Valley—Eagan
(Minnesota) School District

COMPASS POINT BOOKS ✦ MINNEAPOLIS, MINNESOTA

Compass Point Books
3109 West 50th Street, #115
Minneapolis, MN 55410

Visit Compass Point Books on the Internet at *www.compasspointbooks.com*
or e-mail your request to *custserv@compasspointbooks.com*

Editor: Jennifer VanVoorst
Page Production: Heather Griffin
Photo Researcher: Marcie C. Spence
Cartographer: XNR Productions, Inc.
Library Consultant: Kathleen Baxter

Art Director: Jaime Martens
Creative Director: Keith Griffin
Editorial Director: Carol Jones
Managing Editor: Catherine Neitge

Library of Congress Cataloging-in-Publication Data
Dell, Pamela.
  Wilma Mankiller: chief of the Cherokee Nation / by Pamela Dell.
     p. cm. — (Signature lives)
  Includes bibliographical references and index.
  ISBN 0-7565-1600-5 (hard cover)
  1. Mankiller, Wilma Pearl, 1945– 2. Cherokee women—Biography.
  3. Cherokee Indians—Kings and rulers—Biography. 4. Cherokee
Indians—Social conditions.
  I. Title. II. Series.
  E99.C5M333 2006
  975.004'975570092—dc22   2005025218

MODERN AMERICA

Starting in the late 19th century, advancements in all areas of human activity transformed an old world into a new and modern place. Inventions prompted rapid shifts in lifestyle, and scientific discoveries began to alter the way humanity viewed itself. Beginning with World War I, warfare took place on a global scale, and ideas such as nationalism and communism showed that countries were taking a larger view of their place in the world. The combination of all these changes continues to produce what we know as the modern world.

Table of Contents

Chapter

1 THE TRAIL OF TEARS

ༀ᠁᠁ༀ

Wilma Mankiller stood proudly in the tribal council chamber of the Cherokee Nation, dressed in a dark suit and a white blouse. She was the center of attention for a large crowd that included friends and family, tribal council members, reporters, photographers, and many other guests. On this day, December 14, 1985, the 40-year-old Mankiller was making history.

In ancient days, before the influence of European culture, Cherokee women had held prominent and revered roles in all aspects of their society. But no woman had ever held the powerful position of chief of the entire Cherokee Nation. As Mankiller raised her hand and solemnly pledged to fulfill the duties of her new office, she officially became the first woman to serve in the highest office of her people. She was

In 1838, the Cherokee people were forced from their homeland in the Southeast and made to relocate to Indian Territory, in what is now the state of Oklahoma.

chief of the Cherokee Nation.

Wilma Mankiller's story is one of strength and determination and hope. But it is not her story alone, for as she herself has said:

> *Especially in the context of a tribal people, no individual's life stands apart and alone from the rest. My own story has meaning only as long as it is a part of the overall story of my people. For above all else, I am a Cherokee woman.*

With this in mind, the story of Wilma Mankiller begins in 1830. That year, the U.S. Congress passed the Indian Removal Act. This act called for the "Five Civilized Tribes" of the Southeast—the Cherokee, the Chickasaw, the Choctaw, the Seminole, and the Muscogee, or Creek—to be removed from their ancestral native lands so that whites could settle there. The five tribes were to be relocated to a vast wilderness west of the Mississippi River, then known simply as Indian Territory.

Once the act was signed into law, the removal promptly began. Over the next three years,

Today the use of the term Five Civilized Tribes *is often considered negative and condescending. But the whites of the 1700s and 1800s did not consider it so. By then, the five large tribes of the Southeast had absorbed many of the customs and practices of European and U.S. culture, which the whites saw as a positive, "civilized" thing.*

thousands of Native Americans were brutally evicted from their homelands. Hundreds were killed or died of starvation, disease, or exposure to the elements. By 1838, only the Cherokees remained in the Southeast.

That May, the people of the Cherokee Nation received chilling news. The U.S. government was organizing a major military force to remove them from the lands they had inhabited for centuries. Any Cherokee who did not willingly leave by May 23, 1838, was to be forcibly removed.

When the removal deadline arrived, the U.S. troops fell upon the Cherokee villages suddenly and with brute force. With no warning and no time to

The Cherokees traveled over land and by water to reach their new territory.

prepare for the journey, people were dragged from their homes with nothing but the clothes on their backs. Those who resisted being taken were often beaten and sometimes killed on the spot. Old people who moved slowly were sometimes forced along with the point of a bayonet in their back.

The Cherokees were organized into groups to make the difficult trek, over land or by river, to Indian Territory, nearly 1,000 miles (1,600 kilometers) to the west. They traveled west in a series of migrations. The first groups were forced to leave in the last weeks of spring 1838.

Throughout the summer, a burning sun scorched the land. Drought raged, and fresh water was virtually unavailable. Food supplies rotted or were stolen by those paid to deliver them along the way. Diseases of all kinds broke out on the trail as well. Even the strongest soon became weak and exhausted. Groups that set out in the fall had to contend with the frigid winter weather, and freezing ice and snows killed hundreds. Rampant starvation and disease added to the many hardships the Cherokees already faced.

As the Cherokees moved west, their routes were marked by an

As they journeyed westward, many Cherokees refused the U.S. government's offer of clothing and other necessities. This was a means of protesting what was happening to them. Accepting such aid, the Cherokees believed, would send the message that they were willingly leaving their homeland.

increasing number of graves. By March, the last of them were arriving in Indian Territory, the area which in the next century would become the state of Oklahoma.

The trail from their eastern homeland to the western wilderness was a scene of severe human misery. The Cherokees called it *Nunna daul Tsunyi*— the "Trail on Which We Cried," or the "Trail of Tears." Historians differ slightly on estimated numbers,

The Cherokees traveled nearly 1,000 miles (1,600 km) to reach their new homeland.

but most agree that of the nearly 16,000 Cherokees forced off their homelands, approximately a quarter died, escaped, or were unaccounted for at the end of the trail.

Those who survived the Nunna daul Tsunyi found little relief at their destination. The U.S. government had promised the Cherokees food, farming equipment, shelter, and everything else they would need to begin a new life. But like countless other failed promises that had been made to them, this one was empty, too. Still, the Cherokees began to rebuild a nearly destroyed nation in an unfamiliar and unwelcomed land. They kept the flame of Cherokee

A memorial in Conway, Arkansas, marks a site along the Trail of Tears.

culture alive as best they could. That flame, and the great spirit of survival, was passed on as new generations were born in the new land. And from those proud and determined ancestors came many future leaders and Cherokee chiefs.

One of the most remarkable and respected of these was born on November 18, 1945, in Tahlequah, Oklahoma, the seat of the relocated Cherokee Nation. From a poor childhood and a troubled adolescence, Wilma Pearl Mankiller would grow up to dedicate her life to serving the Cherokee people. She would become a powerful leader who would guide the Cherokee Nation to a place of restored self-respect and high national regard. ❧

2 A CHEROKEE CHILDHOOD

❧❦❧

Anyone passing by the house at Mankiller Flats in northeastern Oklahoma's Adair County would not have been impressed. The dense forests surrounding the house teemed with raccoon, deer, wolves, and wildcats. In the leafy branches of pin oaks and hickory trees, woodpeckers and orioles made their nests. But set against this beautiful backdrop, the house itself was nothing much to look at. It was constructed of rough, unpainted planks of wood topped by a tin roof. Beyond the house stood an outhouse, because no bathroom facilities existed inside.

The interior of the house was equally simple. Like the exterior, the walls and floors of its four simple rooms were unfinished wood planks. A woodstove in one of the rooms not only provided heat but was also

Northeastern Oklahoma's Cherokee country is filled with beautiful fields and forests.

used for cooking. The house had no indoor plumbing, running water, telephone service, or even electricity. Water for drinking, cooking, and bathing had to be hauled from the springs a quarter of a mile (0.4 km) away. This was a long way when you were carrying two heavy pails of water.

But none of this mattered to young Wilma Pearl Mankiller. Until 1948, the year of her third birthday, Wilma's family had always rented places to live. But this home—and the land upon which it stood— was theirs. Wilma was happy that her family finally owned their own home.

Like the woods surrounding it, Wilma's house was bursting with life. Her father, Charley Mankiller, was a proud Cherokee directly descended from people who had walked the Trail of Tears more than 100 years earlier. Orphaned at a young age, Charley was sent to an Oklahoma school for Native American children. There, he was made to speak only English and forbidden to use his native Cherokee language. He did well at

Until 1821, the Cherokee language had no alphabet and was only a spoken language. But that year, a Cherokee named Sequoyah created a syllabary, something like an alphabet, which enabled Cherokees to write and read their language. The Cherokee syllabary contains 85 sounds, or syllables, and is very easy to learn because each character represents only a single sound. With the Cherokee syllabary, literacy in the Cherokee Nation grew rapidly. In Indian Territory before 1907, Cherokee literacy surpassed that of their white neighbors.

reading and writing English, but he did not lose his strong connection to his own culture.

As a young man of 21, Charley married Clara Irene Sitton, a white girl of Irish and Dutch descent. Irene, as she was called, had lived in Cherokee country her entire life and had known Charley for much of that time. Still, they had a whirlwind courtship. When they married in 1937, Irene was only 15 years old.

Charley and Irene Mankiller were in love and happy. Soon they began a family. By the time they moved into their home at Mankiller Flats in 1949, they already had three sons and three daughters.

Students at Native American schools were discouraged from speaking their native languages and practicing their native customs.

The eldest was Louis Donald (Don), followed by Frieda Marie, Robert Charles, Frances Kay, John David, and Wilma Pearl—the youngest of the six. She was named Wilma after Charley's aunt and Pearl after Irene's mother. She also had a Cherokee name: *A-ji-luhsgi*, which means "flower." Wilma was an attractive child, with brown hair and hazel eyes. Over the next 12 years, five younger brothers and sisters would join the family: Linda Jean, Richard Colson, Vanessa Lou, James Ray, and William Edward.

Feeding and caring for such a big family was a lot of work for Wilma's parents, but no one ever went hungry. They raised peanuts and strawberries for sale, and they grew beans, corn, and tomatoes in the family vegetable garden. The surrounding woods provided wild onions, walnuts, mushrooms, and lots of other good things to eat. Charley and Don hunted and fished, bringing home wild pig, quail, squirrels, frogs, and many kinds of fish.

Wilma's mother worked hard at home, too, cooking, cleaning, washing, and sewing clothes for her children. Once a year, if the family had enough money, the children would get new winter coats and new leather shoes.

The sizeable Mankiller family had little in the way of material comforts, but for Wilma, it was a cocoon of closeness and love. Her family might not have been able to give her the fine clothes that

Beautiful Lake Tenkiller was not far from the Mankiller home.

some of her classmates wore, but they nurtured her pride and intelligence. She could take these wherever she went.

Their Cherokee heritage was important to the Mankiller family. The family sometimes attended tribal gatherings, where traditional Cherokee ceremonial dances were performed. The dances lasted all night, and Wilma loved the excitement, as well as the chance to stay up late. Occasionally they would attend the local Baptist church, which was encouraged by the whites. But the Mankillers held fast to their native traditions and never truly adopted

Many people enjoy watching or performing traditional Native American dances.

Christianity. To Wilma, except for her own mother, the white people were strange and mystifying. She was wary of them and disappeared as quickly as possible whenever one showed up at their home at Mankiller Flats.

For the first 11 years of her life, Wilma's childhood had been almost idyllic. As a Cherokee, she had learned that all of nature was worthy of respect. She had come to have a deep love and respect for nature—the rocks, the stars, the animals and plants. On stormy days, she loved the sound of the raindrops beating on the tin roof above her head. In the spring, her favorite season, she loved to see the trees burst into bloom and colorful flowers push up from the earth. Mankiller Flats was a beautiful place—one where A-ji-luhsgi, the little Cherokee flower, expected to stay forever. But difficult times were coming. Soon all of this beauty would become a distant memory.

From the time the United States was founded, its government had made many promises to the Cherokee people. In 1835, the U.S. Congress had signed a treaty with the Cherokees that read in part:

> *The United States hereby ... agree that the land ceded to the Cherokee nation ... [will never] be included within the territorial limits ... of any state or territory.*

But time and time again those promises had been broken. When the Native Americans relocated to Indian Territory, they had been assured that this land would be theirs forevermore. But as white settlers pushed farther and farther west, they again began encroaching on lands that had been reserved for the Native Americans.

In 1887, Congress passed the Dawes Act, which called for Indian land to be divided up and parceled out to individual families. This forced the Cherokees, who believed that land could not be owned, to live in ways that went against their culture and beliefs. But this meant little to the government or those eager to homestead.

Each Cherokee family was allotted 160 acres (64 hectares). A single adult individual was granted 80 acres (32 hectares). The vast acreage of Cherokee and other Indian land that remained went to white settlers. Over several years, the stealing of Native American lands was accomplished through numerous "land runs" in Indian Territory. By 1907, white takeover erased Indian Territory from the map for good. In its place came the state of Oklahoma.

This was not, however, the end of the government's attempts to disintegrate Cherokee culture. In the 1950s, the U.S. government began implementing new methods to deal with what they called the "Indian problem." And the peaceful, happy life that Wilma had known began to come undone.

In Washington, D.C., the Bureau of Indian Affairs had decided that Native Americans would fare better if they were integrated into the everyday life of American society. They set up a relocation program that strongly encouraged—and in many cases forced—Native American families to move to the

A land rush at the end of the 19th century brought white settlers to the new Indian Territory.

country's large cities, such as Chicago, San Francisco, New York, and Detroit. The U.S. government promised to help them move and resettle by providing housing and jobs.

Some of these government officials came to the Mankiller home to explain the details of the program to Charley and Irene. They brought colorful brochures that promoted the relocation program by showing supposedly happy, smiling Indians and wonderful homes. At first, Charley resisted the idea of relocating his family. He wanted to remain in his homeland, near his relatives and close to the land of his ancestors.

But Mankiller Flats, like the rest of the region, had been in the grip of a two-year drought. The family's cash crops were virtually gone, and Charley could barely provide for his wife and many children. The government painted him a picture of a happy family and a decent home in a city full of job opportunities and good schools. The Mankillers faced a difficult decision.

Leaving the life they had always known would be hard for everyone, but Charley and Irene wanted to do what they felt was best for their still-growing family. In October 1956, a month before Wilma's 11th birthday, the Mankillers packed up their meager belongings and caught a train heading west out of Oklahoma.

Traveling to California, Wilma had feelings similar to those expressed more than 100 years earlier by George Hicks, one of the Cherokee leaders on the Trail of Tears. Upon leaving the Southeast, he said:

We are now about to take our leave and kind farewell to our native land. … It is with sorrow that we are forced by the authority of the white man to quit the scenes of our childhood. … We bid a final farewell to it and all we hold dear.

Map showing the United States, with Canada to the north, Mexico to the south, the Pacific Ocean and Atlantic Ocean. Inset maps show San Francisco area (Pacific Ocean, Alcatraz Island, Oakland, San Francisco, Riverbank) and the Cherokee Nation area (Adair County, Tahlequah (capital of Cherokee Nation), Oklahoma City, Mankiller Flats, Bell). Fayetteville is marked near the Oklahoma-Arkansas border.

Leaving everything they knew, the family traveled 1,500 miles (2,400 km) to San Francisco, California.

Wilma had never been farther than 10 miles (16 km) from home. During the two days and two nights she sat on the train, she cried more than once. As an adult, she remembered that day as the beginning of her family's own Trail of Tears, one from which she hoped someday to return. ❧

Wilma considered the trip from Oklahoma to California to be her own Trail of Tears.

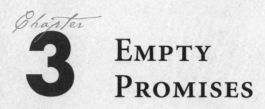

Chapter

3 EMPTY PROMISES

❦

"Wilma Mankiller!" Roll call at school was always painful for the young girl in a new city where everything was unfamiliar and often frightening. Each time a teacher called out her name, the other kids laughed, as if her name were some kind of joke. In rural Oklahoma, where the name was well-known, no one had ever made fun of it. But in San Francisco, Wilma's classmates found it immensely funny that a girl would have the name "Mankiller."

Being laughed at was a new and humiliating experience, but Wilma was proud to bear her family name. It was one of the most respected names in the entire history of Cherokee culture and had been the family surname for five generations, including her own.

The bustling, crowded city of San Francisco was an unwelcome change of scenery for Wilma Mankiller.

In the earliest times, however, it had not been anyone's last name. According to Cherokee legend and history, there were two kinds of *Asgay-dihi*, or mankiller. The first referred to a military rank or position of power, just as the title "captain" did. A mankiller was one who protected a Cherokee village, and each village had its own. A mankiller was a fierce warrior who had risen to his respected position by his own brave deeds.

Another kind of Cherokee mankiller was more like a shaman. This mankiller was believed to have special powers, and his job was to punish those who had done someone wrong. He was said to have the power to make a sick person worse or to shoot invisible arrows at an enemy or wrongdoer.

But in 1950s San Francisco, few if any knew the honored history of this name. It was only one of many painful difficulties for Wilma and her family as they tried to adjust to life in the city. The family had left a strong community and many relatives behind. One who

Each Cherokee person belongs to one of seven clans, or groups of people related by a common ancestor. In past times, each clan was responsible for certain tasks. The Wolf Clan were warriors who protected the village. The Deer Clan were hunters, while the Wild Potato Clan gathered plants and taught their knowledge. The Bird Clan served as messengers. The Long Hair Clan kept and taught the village's history and traditions. The Paint Clan were medicine people, while the Blue Clan were medicine people just for children. The Mankiller family is a member of the Blue Clan.

The flyer

A Cherokee
shaman, or
healer, was
often called
a mankiller.

had not come with them was Wilma's eldest sister,
Frieda, who wanted to finish high school there. Still,
San Francisco was near Riverbank, the rural

community where Grandma Sitton, Irene's mother, now lived. One relative living fairly close by was better than none.

City life was a shock for the Mankiller family. They had been promised an apartment by the government and had been given vouchers to use for buying groceries. But they had never even heard of many of the everyday city foods, and there were no apartments ready for them. Instead, they were shuffled off to a cheap hotel in the city's Tenderloin district for their first two weeks in town.

As one of the worst neighborhoods in San Francisco, the Tenderloin was home to drug dealers and prostitutes. Homeless people slept in doorways, and glass from broken liquor bottles littered the sidewalks. Lost and bewildered, Wilma longed to hear the sounds of nature at night instead of fistfights and screaming sirens.

Still, this difficult time offered Wilma many new and exciting experiences. One of the strangest things she had ever seen occurred early on. Standing in the hotel's hallway one day, she saw the wall slide open to reveal a box. Several people who had been standing in the hall got into the box and the wall closed again. A few minutes later, the wall opened once more. Now, entirely different people walked out of the box. This was Wilma's first encounter with an elevator. She soon experienced many other new things as well, including learning how to roller-skate, ride a bike, and use a telephone.

The move to a small apartment in the working-class neighborhood of Potrero Hill improved things—but not much. The space was tight for the large Mankiller family, now with one more on the way, and money was scarce. Wilma's father and oldest brother took work in a factory that made rope. But even with two paychecks, the family barely survived. That first year in San Francisco, 1956, James was born. The last Mankiller child, William,

Children cluster around a collapsed house in San Francisco's run-down Potrero Hill neighborhood.

was born in 1961.

The Mankillers tried their best to build a community with other Cherokees in the city, but it was hard to do. Life was a constant struggle, and there was not even the land to help provide for their needs. Most Indians remained on the fringes of society, often living in slum neighborhoods, with few of the opportunities the government had led them to expect. Instead of escaping from poverty and misery, Charley Mankiller's family found life in California even worse.

For Wilma, life was especially difficult. Her classmates at school looked down on her for being different. It wasn't so much her family's poverty, because others were poor, too. It was the way she dressed. It was the strange accent in her speech. She felt disliked and alone. Much of the time she felt afraid, unsure of herself, and rebellious, with no place to hide in the chaotic city sprawl. So instead of trying to find a hiding place where she was, Wilma ran away.

At least five times in the years before she started high school, Wilma hopped on a bus and rode to Riverbank and the serenity of Grandma Sitton's rural home. Each time, her grandmother called Wilma's parents, and Charley would come and bring his daughter home. Finally, understanding how unhappy Wilma was in the city, Charley and Irene agreed that she could spend her eighth-grade year with her grandmother. By then, Grandma Sitton had moved in with her son, his wife, and their children at their home on a dairy farm.

This change of scene was a positive one for young Wilma. In that stable, peaceful environment, she began to feel more happy and confident. She made friends and started liking herself better. The next fall, Wilma rejoined her family, who had moved to a rough

Rural California brought a refreshing change of scenery for Wilma.

San Francisco neighborhood called Hunter's Point. She willingly enrolled at a San Francisco high school, but she quickly discovered that the inner-city school experience had not improved for her. The school she attended was rough as well, and there were many violent incidents among the students. In class, Wilma felt bored, disliked, and alone. She had no idea what she would do after high school, and her grades were only good in the few classes that interested her.

Wilma never really felt at home in the Hunter's Point housing project.

The only really enjoyable moments she experienced were after school and on weekends, when

she escaped to the San Francisco Indian Center. At the center, in the city's Mission district, Wilma made friends with other Indian teens. Many of them had also come from Oklahoma under the relocation program, so they understood her feelings, frustrations, and problems. At the Indian Center, she enjoyed social events like dances, sports, and just hanging out. It was the place of refuge she had been seeking since she had left Oklahoma.

Still unsure of who she was and where her life was going, Wilma made the Indian Center the focal point of her teenage world. Meanwhile, she waited impatiently for June 1963. For Wilma, that month of that year marked the moment of her escape. In June 1963, she would graduate from high school. ❧

Wilma's involvement with the San Francisco Indian Center helped her adjust to life in San Francisco. It provided entertainment and social and cultural activities for youths, as well as a place for adults to hold powwows and discuss matters of importance with other Native Americans who had been relocated. Wilma recalled, "There was something at the Center for everyone. It was a safe place to go, even if we only wanted to hang out." Though she was far from Cherokee country, the center helped reinforce Wilma's identity as a Cherokee and her understanding of Cherokee history and traditions.

4 FINDING HER CAUSE

୧୦⟨×⟩୧୦

For the Mankiller family, the idea of pursuing a higher education was about as realistic as flying a spaceship to the moon. No Mankiller had ever gone on to college, and Wilma had never even given the idea a thought. Instead, after graduating from high school, she moved out of her parents' home and in with her older sister Frances. She was hired by a finance company to work in its office doing filing and making telephone calls to delinquent loan holders. And before she even turned 18, Wilma got married.

Wilma had met her future husband, who was four years older than she, at a Latino dance. Hector Hugo Olaya de Bardi, or Hugo, came from Ecuador. To the young, impressionable teenager, Hugo seemed worldly and sophisticated. He had classy manners,

A Native American girl involved in the 1969 takeover of Alcatraz Island publicly asserts her people's claim to the land.

39 ୨୦

and his dark, handsome looks attracted her immediately. Wilma had barely been out of her own neighborhood, but Hugo drove his own car and exposed her to a wide range of new cultural experiences within the city—people and places she had not even known existed. After a long day at work, Wilma was thrilled to be escorted by the dashing Olaya to a nice restaurant or an exciting dance club. Olaya was enrolled in college, too, and planned to make something of himself in the world.

After a breathless summer in a social whirl, Wilma agreed to marry Hugo. In November 1963, just days before her 18th birthday, she and Hugo caught a bus for Reno, Nevada. With no family members present, they married in a wedding chapel there. Then they took another bus to enjoy a honeymoon in Chicago.

When the young couple returned to San Francisco, they lived with Hugo's relatives before getting their own home. Wilma continued working and took care of the cooking and cleaning while Hugo went to class by day and worked at night.

Wilma soon discovered that she was pregnant, and in August 1964, the couple's daughter Felicia was born. In June 1966, Wilma gave birth to their second daughter, Gina.

Wilma was now most often known as Mrs. Hugo Olaya. Not even 21 years old yet, she had a husband, two children, a home, and a job. But the job was not challenging, and the day-in, day-out routine of her life barely changed. As she tried to fulfill the traditional role of wife and mother, Wilma felt more and more discontented. All around her the city was exploding with revolutionary ideas and worthwhile causes in which to take an interest. People were experimenting with alternative lifestyles and staging protests against rigid university policies, racial discrimination, and the war in Vietnam. The air around her was restless

San Francisco students gathered to peacefully protest the Vietnam War.

Members of the American Indian Movement picketed to raise awareness for their cause.

with the energy of change, but Wilma's own world seemed to be closing in. As the months passed, the stifling routine of her married existence made Wilma think more and more about what she really wanted in life. And as time went on, Wilma and Hugo began to grow farther and farther apart.

In the late 1960s, Wilma took a big step toward the independence she now longed for. She enrolled at Skyline Junior College, in a suburb of San Francisco. Although she had hated everything about school as a teen, she realized that becoming more educated was necessary if she was to enlarge her world. She signed up for classes that included sociology, literature, and criminal justice. She did well and was surprised to find college life much more enjoyable than any schooling she had had before.

Gaining confidence, Wilma transferred to San Francisco State University, enrolling through an educational-opportunity program for minorities. Once she got her footing in this larger, more intensely academic school, she thrived. Soon, she was thinking about the opportunities that might lie ahead, beyond her life as a married woman. She later wrote about this time:

> *I wanted to set my own limits and control my destiny. I began to have dreams about more freedom and independence, and I finally came to understand that I did not have to live a life based on someone else's dream.*

As Wilma continued her college education and gained confidence, her sights shifted farther out into her community. She again sought out the Indian Center, the place that had provided refuge during the turmoil of her teenage years. Soon

As the 1970s loomed, Native Americans across the nation were becoming active in the fight for civil rights. In 1968, an organization known as the American Indian Movement, or AIM, was founded in Minnesota. Its purpose was to bring awareness to the American public about important Native American issues. Chapters of AIM organized demonstrations and sit-ins to bring attention to age-old grievances. They publicized issues such as what many considered the legalized theft by whites of tribal lands and other valuable resources.

she was swept into the spirited atmosphere there and thinking more about Native American rights and issues than she ever had before.

But then disaster struck that refuge. On the night of October 28, 1969, the San Francisco Indian Center burned to the ground. The cause of the four-alarm fire was never absolutely determined, but some suspected arson. Fed up with social injustice, the city's Native American community rushed to organize a demonstration that would get the nation's attention. They decided to take over Alcatraz Island, or "The Rock."

The Rock, a huge stone island in San Francisco Bay, had been used by Native Americans since long before whites had arrived in the West. Later, because of its remote location, the U.S. government had built Alcatraz Prison there. Since the prison's closure in 1963, San Francisco's board of supervisors had been busy trying to find a good and profitable use for it. Finally, they had accepted a proposal to build a huge tourist complex, complete with shopping mall, on the island.

The country's Native Americans objected to its use in this way. To them, Alcatraz was a small symbol of all the North American land they had lost to white Americans. So, on November 9, 1969, 14 Native Americans made their way across the cold and choppy waters of the bay to claim Alcatraz in

the name of Indians of all tribes. This takeover—
and an earlier one that had happened in 1964—was
based on an agreement known as the Fort Laramie
Treaty of 1868. According to that document, any
Native American male 18 or older could petition to
homestead on any unused or abandoned federal land
if his tribe had been involved at the time the treaty
was created.

A group of Native Americans claimed Alcatraz Island on behalf of all native tribes.

The takeover of Alcatraz was a highly symbolic

move, and as part of the protest, the occupiers made a symbolic gesture to buy the island from the U.S. government. They offered the government red cloth and glass beads that had a total value of $24. This, they felt, was a fitting offer, considering that white men had purchased New York's Manhattan Island for the same price 300 years earlier.

But they had barely set foot on land before they were removed by the U.S. Coast Guard. Early on November 20, 1969, however, they returned as a larger group. Eighty-nine native men, women, and children again took possession of Alcatraz, this time outfitted with sleeping bags, cooking equipment, food, and water. Over the following days, more and more Native Americans, from tribes all over the country, came to join the protesters.

Wilma's brother Richard was the first in the Mankiller family to become part of the Alcatraz demonstration. Vanessa and James soon followed. Finally, when Linda and her children decided to journey out to

> *The takeover of Alcatraz had a profound and historic effect. It shone a huge spotlight on American Indian issues, causing the American public in general and the federal government in particular to finally take serious notice. It also fostered within Native Americans a new and powerful sense of pride in their heritage and their place within the fabric of the United States. In the end, the takeover at Alcatraz spawned hundreds of other related demonstrations throughout the following decade.*

Some Native Americans erected traditional housing for their stay on Alcatraz.

the island, Wilma went with them. It was a decision that would radically affect the rest of her life.

By taking a stand at Alcatraz, Wilma had become part of a symbolic demonstration that riveted the attention of the entire country. For her, it was a life-changing episode. At Alcatraz, Wilma discovered who she was and where she was going. She had finally found her path. ❧

5 RETURN TO TRIBAL LAND

❧✦❧

The car was a little red Mazda. It was not fancy or expensive. But for Wilma Mankiller Olaya, it was a symbol of her own independence. She was now leading two lives—one as student and community activist and the other as wife and mother. She was learning and growing. The work she was doing outside her home made her feel more fulfilled and powerful than ever before.

Hugo, however, was not at all happy about his wife's outside activities, and he flatly refused to allow her to get a car. But Wilma was not about to stop what had become her life-giving activities, despite Hugo's attempts to control her. She needed a car to get from one place to another in the city. She was determined to attend tribal events in other places as

Wilma Mankiller (center) is a member of the Cherokee people's Blue Clan. In Cherokee tradition, this clan's job was to serve as medicine people just for children.

well. In an act of defiance, Wilma withdrew money from the bank and bought herself the Mazda without Hugo's knowledge.

The car was a symbol, but its main purpose was practical. Now she had the opportunity to experience many things that she had not had access to before. Since Alcatraz, she had become deeply interested in the changes occurring in society, and she wanted to be a part of them. With a car she was free to go to plays, concerts, political events, and women's rights demonstrations, and she now did all of these.

The Pit River Indians, whose tribal lands are located north of San Francisco, were fighting a legal battle against the huge and powerful Pacific Gas & Electric Corporation. The tribe wanted to be lawfully acknowledged as the rightful owners of millions of acres of their ancestral territory that PG&E had claimed. Mankiller worked with the Pit River tribe until she moved away from the Bay Area.

More importantly, Wilma took a job as the director of the Native American Youth Center in Oakland, across the bay from San Francisco. There she helped establish after-school programs for Indian students. She sought out literacy programs for teens who couldn't read well and arranged field trips to out-of-town tribal events. On top of all this, she found time to volunteer with the Pit River Indians, too.

As Wilma became increasingly involved with Native American causes, she began to see how pride in their Native American heritage

The intake bay at the Pit River Power Plant is part of the land claimed by the Pit River Indians.

empowered her people. She believed that even those living in poverty in the cities' worst neighborhoods could survive with dignity if they honored their cultural roots. She saw that her work was to help increase this pride and to do whatever else she could to change and improve things within the Native

American community.

Wilma traveled often to meet with tribal leaders and elders, and she frequently brought her young daughters along. She began to acquire a deep understanding of international law, treaty rights, legal defense funds, and much more. And with every trip and every encounter, her understanding of the history and culture of tribes native to California and elsewhere increased. Wilma remembered:

> *All of the people I encountered—the militants, the wise elders, the keepers of the medicine, the storytellers—were my teachers, my best teachers. I knew my education would never be complete. In a way, it was only beginning. I felt like a newborn whose eyes have just opened to the first light.*

At home, however, things had reached a point of serious meltdown. Wilma was devoted to her two daughters, and she wanted her marriage to work. But to give up her new, energizing life would be like agreeing to suffocate. By 1973, she and Hugo were barely a part of each other's worlds.

During the time of the Alcatraz occupation,

The state of California is home to dozens of Native American tribes. Among the best-known are the Miwok, Chumash, Shoshone, Paiute, and Shasta tribes. At the time Europeans arrived in what is now the United States, California was the most densely populated of the current states with a population of approximately 150,000.

Wilma's father had died, and she and her brothers and sisters had returned to Mankiller Flats to bury him in the land of his forefathers. While there, Wilma had felt the pull of the land. Powerful memories of her childhood in Oklahoma surfaced again. She began to think more and more of returning there and re-establishing her roots in a permanent way.

The first step in her plan to return was to leave Hugo. Wilma asked him for a divorce in 1974, and he eventually agreed. She moved across the bay to Oakland, where it was less expensive to live as a single mother with two daughters. To confirm her new identity, Wilma dropped her husband's name of Olaya. She again became Wilma Mankiller.

Mankiller worked hard over the next year. She continued to volunteer with the Pit River Indians, and she took a job doing social work for the Urban Indian Resource Center. She needed to save enough money to make the move with Felicia and Gina to Oklahoma, and this goal was the driving force behind everything she did.

The summer of 1976 arrived, but Mankiller was not yet prepared to move. Instead, she arranged a trip back to Mankiller Flats so

> *The Achomawi tribe is often referred to as the Pit River Indians in part because the tribe's historic land was located in the drainage of the Pit River in northeastern California. The name* Pit River *came from the tribe's practice of digging pits for the purpose of catching game.*

she could reacquaint herself with the area over a longer time. She found a rustic cabin to live in near ceremonial dance grounds, and she and her two daughters settled in. At 10 and 12, Felicia and Gina did not adjust instantly to living in a house that had no running water. But for Wilma, the weeks in Oklahoma were rich and satisfying.

She enlivened old friendships and took her girls to many tribal events. Ceremonial dances were a favorite pastime. Gathered at the ceremonial grounds, everyone ate the abundant foods of summer, chatted, and engaged in traditional Cherokee sports such as archery and stickball. The highlight of the evening was the traditional dances themselves, which often

Cherokee girls compete in a traditional game of stickball.

went on until dawn. Mankiller knew she would soon return permanently to the land of her childhood.

In the summer of 1977, with $20 in her pocket and a rental truck filled with her belongings, Mankiller and her daughters made the permanent move back to Oklahoma. She had brought little with her besides a few personal possessions and her unshakable determination to find a way to support her family. At Mankiller Flats, no trace was left of the home she had lived in as a child. But the land was still there, beautiful and rich with flowers, trees, and animals. She knew she could rebuild.

But first Mankiller needed a job. Her mother, Irene, had recently moved back to Adair County herself. Now, Mankiller and her daughters moved into Irene's home. Mankiller immediately set out looking for work. In her free time, she cooked and sewed and played the guitar that Hugo had once bought her.

Finding work was difficult. She hoped to continue her work as an Indian activist, but she was frequently turned down for being overqualified. The long search was frustrating, but in the fall of 1977, she finally met with success. Mankiller was hired at $11,000 a year as an economic stimulus coordinator for the Cherokee Nation of Oklahoma. Her duties focused on spurring Native American college students to study environmental health and science and then to use that knowledge to improve their communities.

Mankiller quickly found that her experience working for Native American causes was invaluable. She excelled at writing grant proposals, some of which led to funding for the Cherokee tribe. Her success impressed Chief Ross Swimmer, the elected head of the Cherokee Nation, and his council members. But Mankiller herself felt bogged down by the slow and bureaucratic way things got done within the Cherokee Nation administration. After all her grassroots activities in San Francisco, she hoped to kindle the same kind of energies again.

By 1979, Mankiller was working as a program development specialist for the Cherokee Nation. She was building a new home at Mankiller Flats and was pleased with the outcome of her move back to the state. But one thing was still undone: She had never finished her undergraduate college degree before leaving San Francisco. That year, she decided to go back to school.

Mankiller eventually received a bachelor's degree in social sciences and a master's degree in community planning from the University of Arkansas.

With just a few courses left to finish her bachelor's degree, Mankiller enrolled in graduate school at the University of Arkansas in Fayetteville, a little more than an hour's drive from home. She planned to get a graduate degree in community planning, a move that

gave her a sense of optimism. Everything was working out amazingly well. She had money to live on through grants and graduate education assistantships. She had been assured that her job at the Cherokee Nation would be waiting for her whenever she wanted to return to it. She had a long drive to school each day, but it was valuable time for planning her future. Little did Mankiller know it as she began attending the University of Arkansas, but very dark days were coming. She would meet them just over the next hill. ℘

6 A BRUSH WITH DEATH

Chapter

ৎ৵৵৶৶

he night of November 8, 1979, there was a terrible rustling in the trees outside Wilma Mankiller's home. The November winds pushed across the valley, stirring the grasses and the plants. Dark clouds scudded across the sky. But it was not the wind that was creating the strange disturbing noise. It was not clouds that formed the spooky shapes that seemed to encircle the Mankiller house. It was the owls.

That night, seemingly hundreds of owls shivered in the trees surrounding the house. The dark sky was filled with them as they flew and flocked. The owls' eerie voices rose into the dark, chilly air in a haunting chorus.

Where the owls came from that night no one could tell. There had never been an earlier incident

Wilma Mankiller took the Cherokee practice of "being of good mind" to heart: She was able to face death and come back smiling.

of such a thing. But the birds brought with them a sense of foreboding. Mankiller had never been very frightened by owls. But she came from a native tradition that saw these birds as the messengers of bad luck, sometimes even of death, and she knew the stories well. The Cherokee *dedonsek* was a person who could change his shape into the form of an owl, sailing through the night carrying bad luck to whomever it chose. The dedonsek, the bringer of "bad medicine," was someone a Cherokee naturally thought of when he or she heard the ghostly sounds

In Cherokee legend, the owl is a symbol of bad luck, suffering, and death.

of an owl's song.

The owls flocked close to the house that night, and they would not keep quiet. Mankiller went to bed feeling ill at ease. She was not a superstitious person and had no premonition that bad luck was on its way. But why had there been so many owls so close to her home?

The next morning, Mankiller decided to go to Tahlequah, where the Cherokee Nation had its headquarters. She wanted to see about getting some part-time work to supplement her income. Traveling on a two-lane back road, she was only a few miles from home when death suddenly drew near. As her car ascended a hill, she could not see the oncoming traffic. An oncoming car that had been trying to pass a slower vehicle was still in Mankiller's lane. Just as she crested the hill, the two cars violently collided head-on.

Mankiller was hauled, barely conscious, from her destroyed automobile. As the ambulance rushed Mankiller to the hospital in nearby Stillwell, she felt certain she was dying. But the experience was far

In Cherokee lore, the owl most feared as a bringer of death was the tsgili, *or great horned owl. This owl has razor-sharp talons, a wing-span of up to 4 ½ feet (1.4 meters), and vision that is 35 times sharper than human sight. It has special feathers on its wings that allow it to be completely silent in flight, so that its prey never hears it approaching. These physical attributes, coupled with the fact that the bird is active at night, suggest why the* tsgili *was associated with "dark powers."*

from a bad one. She remembered:

> *I experienced a tremendous sense of peace-fulness and warmth. It was a feeling that was better than anything that had ever happened to me. ... As a result of that experience I have lost any fear of death. I began to think of death as walking into spirit country rather than as a frightening event.*

Road signs in Tahlequah, Oklahoma, are printed in both Cherokee and English.

The driver of the other car died on the way to the hospital. That driver, who had also been alone

in her car, was a woman named Sherry Morris. She had been one of Mankiller's closest friends.

Mankiller's recuperation was slow and painful. The front of the car had been rammed so far back by the impact that a part of the hood had gashed her neck. She had broken ribs, a broken left leg and ankle, and the bones in both her face and her right leg had been crushed. During the more than eight weeks that she spent in the hospital, surgeons worked to put her face and right leg back together. After her initial release from the hospital, Mankiller had to return many more times. In all, she endured a total of 17 surgeries and defied predictions that she would never walk again.

But if the owls that had surrounded her that November night were bringing bad luck, all of it had not yet come. In early 1980, her body began to weaken. Soon she could barely use her arms or legs. It was a struggle even to keep her eyes open. It took several months before she discovered what the problem was. She had myasthenia gravis, a form of muscular dystrophy.

> *The Cherokees attempt to cultivate an approach to life that they call "being of good mind." They try to take a positive attitude toward even negative life experiences and use such experiences to grow and improve their lot in life. Holding to this ideal, Mankiller turned her car-accident ordeal into an experience that helped her later in life. By doing so, she realized that she "had found the way to be of good mind."*

More determined than ever to get back to her active, full life, Mankiller underwent surgery yet again, this time to remove her thymus gland. The operation was successful, and she began to regain her strength almost immediately. Now that she had fought and won some major battles of her own, Mankiller's thoughts returned to helping others.

By 1981, Mankiller was back at her job at the Cherokee Nation. Her confrontation with death had left her confident that she could survive anything. With newfound courage and determination, she stepped up to tasks that before her accident she would never have tackled. In her first year back, she helped to found the Cherokee Nation Community Development Department. She was convinced that the best way to restore Cherokee pride was to allow people to accomplish things themselves, within their individual communities. This new organization was created to help that happen. Mankiller became its first director.

One of the first projects the Community Development Department took on was helping the small and poverty-stricken community of Bell, Oklahoma, rebuild itself. The town residents, 95 percent of whom were Cherokee, took the improvements into their own hands and greatly revitalized their community. With Mankiller's guidance, they refurbished old homes and built

25 solar-powered homes. They laid 16 miles (26 km) of water pipeline, bringing running water to many homes for the first time. The community effort was so successful that it received national media coverage—including a "before and after" story on CBS news.

Tahlequah, Oklahoma, is home of the Cherokee Nation head-quarters.

Mankiller could not have been more proud to see her "self-help" philosophy working so well. The Bell project proved that her people could accomplish great things independently, without outsiders making decisions for them. But the project benefited Mankiller in a more personal way as well. Through the Bell project, Mankiller formed a strong friendship with her co-organizer, a full-blooded Cherokee named Charlie Lee Soap. Over the years, their friendship deepened, and in 1986, the two married. But this time Mankiller retained her last name.

In the early 1980s, that name grew in importance around the Cherokee Nation headquarters. The Bell project had given Mankiller, as its lead organizer, the chance to have a powerful impact on the fortunes of her tribe. She loved helping her community and continually asked the tribal chief, Ross Swimmer, for more of this kind of work. Her competence and easy authority did not go unnoticed. By 1983, Swimmer had been chief for two terms and was preparing to run for re-election once again. Needing a strong candidate for deputy chief to run with him, Swimmer asked Mankiller to be his running mate.

This invitation took Mankiller, only 38 years old, completely by surprise. The Cherokee Nation at that time consisted of about 75,000 citizens. It had its own congress and constitution, and candidates operated political campaigns just as U.S. politicians do. She had never imagined herself in a high national office, nor in any political office at all for that matter.

Mankiller felt highly honored that Swimmer respected her abilities enough to even suggest this possibility, but stepping into the role of deputy chief seemed out of the question. At first, Mankiller

declined, but then she reconsidered. If she refused this opportunity, how could she ever complain that the Cherokee Nation administration was not doing enough? She went back to Swimmer and accepted the challenge of being his running mate. ❧

Ross Swimmer served as chief of the Cherokee Nation for three terms.

7 CHIEF OF A NATION

Chapter

ভ৹১৯

The fight to win the 1983 election had been a difficult one. Mankiller was shocked to find that those who opposed her as deputy chief weren't concerned about her political views on the national level. They were not paying much attention to the platform of ideas she was promoting. The thing they most objected to was that she was a woman.

The idea that a woman should have the responsibility of such a high post was unheard of in the Cherokee Nation. During her campaign, Mankiller was the object of death threats, hate mail, and verbal attacks. But throughout the campaign, she remained poised and her message positive. Despite her foes, all the good she had done within the community had brought her many supporters as well. She had faced

As chief of the Cherokee Nation, Wilma Mankiller met with many important U.S. officials, including President Ronald Reagan.

From 1917 until 1971, the U.S. government —specifically the president—took charge of appointing Cherokee chiefs. During these years, the United States refused to recognize nearly all the chiefs democratically elected by the Cherokees themselves. Finally, in 1971, this practice ended and the U.S. government agreed to recognize tribally elected Cherokee chiefs.

down many difficult challenges in her life with great courage and determination. This one was no different.

That determination paid off. Swimmer and Mankiller won the election, and on August 14, 1983, Wilma Mankiller became the first female deputy chief of the Cherokee Nation. In her new role, she supervised more than 40 different Cherokee Nation programs operating in a total of 14 northeastern Oklahoma counties. She administered and advised on programs for daycare and elder care, community building and maintenance projects, education and literacy, and more.

In 1985, Swimmer announced that he would be taking a national position as head of the Bureau of Indian Affairs. The Cherokee Constitution dictated that the deputy chief take over as chief in such a situation. Mankiller would be making history again, this time as the first female chief of the Cherokee Nation.

Mankiller knew that with this great honor came great responsibility. On December 14, 1985, when she was sworn in as the new chief, she felt the pressure

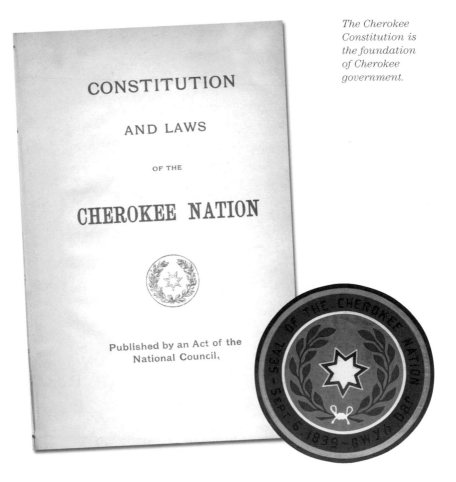

The Cherokee Constitution is the foundation of Cherokee government.

of taking Swimmer's place. She was taking on the role of chief only two years into her four-year term as deputy chief. Furthermore, the Cherokee people had not actually elected her to this highest position of power. Rather, she had inherited the job. She fully expected to meet the same negativity and resistance she had while running for deputy chief. But to her surprise there was no big outcry. Although some of

Wilma Mankiller was 40 years old when she first became chief.

her administration did not wholly support her, she was able to make progress over the next two years. She gained respect in the community and among the council members as well.

By the end of those two years, with election time looming, Mankiller considered entering the race for chief. If she were to win, it would be an undeniable sign that the Cherokee community approved of her as a leader. Mankiller decided to run.

Mankiller's decision to run for chief was

prompted in part by those who doubted she could win. Many, convinced she could never do better than deputy chief, even visited her at home to talk her out of running. But rather than bringing her down, these outside doubters made Mankiller more resolved than ever to rise to the challenge. Once she was chief, she wrote about this experience:

> *I would look out the window and see them coming down the dirt road. ... Finally, I told Charlie that if one more family came down that road and told me not to run, I was going to run for sure. That is just what happened.*

Mankiller had three opponents in the race, and the negative campaigning again swirled around her. But she never lowered herself to respond in the same way. She took the grassroots approach she always had. She visited people in her community and found out what they were thinking and what was bothering them. She took time to get to know them and allow them to learn more about her and what she wanted to bring to the office of chief.

When the 1987 election was held, none of the four candidates for chief received the 50 percent majority needed to win. But with 45 percent of the vote, Mankiller was closest. She and the next-highest contender, a man named

Perry Wheeler, had to compete in a second election. When all the votes from this second election were counted, the winner was clear. Wilma Mankiller had been fairly and unquestionably elected as chief of the Cherokee Nation.

In the summer of 1987, Mankiller was sworn in as chief of the Cherokee Nation for the second time. But for the first time since she had entered politics, taking authority was a joyful experience. When she had taken over from Swimmer in 1985, the people had not directly chosen her. This time she finally had a clear mandate to direct the nation.

Mankiller defined the role of the Cherokee Nation administration as being, more than anything else, a resource for the people. Her concept of how the central government should function was different from that of most other Native American governments. She believed the best way for her people to gain self-respect and pride was to put each Cherokee community in charge of its own change. Under her administration, each individual

Before Mankiller became chief, the U.S. government had traditionally been deeply involved in Cherokee tribal matters, through the Bureau of Indian Affairs (BIA). But in 1990, she achieved a historic milestone in tribal self-governance. She signed an agreement with the BIA that gave the Cherokees and five other tribes full responsibility for overseeing the use of $6.1 million in funds. Up until that point, the BIA had been exclusively in charge of how this money would be spent.

community would take responsibility for planning, building, and maintaining projects that would improve the lives of its people. These communities would look to the central government as a facilitator in successfully accomplishing the projects and improvements they determined for themselves. These projects would include things like developing waterworks, building schools and clinics, and much more.

Getting tribal communities to begin taking the lead in making a difference in the quality of life was

Mankiller's administration helped bring new and modern schools to the Cherokee Nation.

In 1989, Mankiller met with Choctaw Chief Philip Martin.

a difficult task. The idea was virtually unheard-of among other Native American tribes. But Mankiller had always had deep faith in this approach. Over the four years of her first full term as chief, changes started to occur at every level. New energy infused the nation as Cherokees began to demonstrate their vast ability to do what needed to be done. Over and over, they proved they could make their own lives better if given the opportunity.

In 1991, Cherokee Nation elections came again. This time, Mankiller felt no hesitation in putting in her bid for reelection as chief. During the six years she had already spent in office, she had made a major impact on the way the Cherokee people viewed themselves and what they saw themselves capable of. The Cherokee Nation had truly been revitalized. But there was much work still to be done. Mankiller wanted to be the one to continue to guide that process.

Once again, election results showed that her people agreed she was the one for the job. In a stunning victory, Mankiller captured 82.7 percent of the vote. On August 14, 1991, she began her second full term as chief. 🐾

Many of the community development programs Mankiller helped create through the Cherokee Nation relied on the ideas, knowledge, and labor of tribe members themselves. Mankiller said that her experiences in California and Oklahoma had taught her that "poor people have a much, much greater capacity for solving their own problems than most people give them credit for."

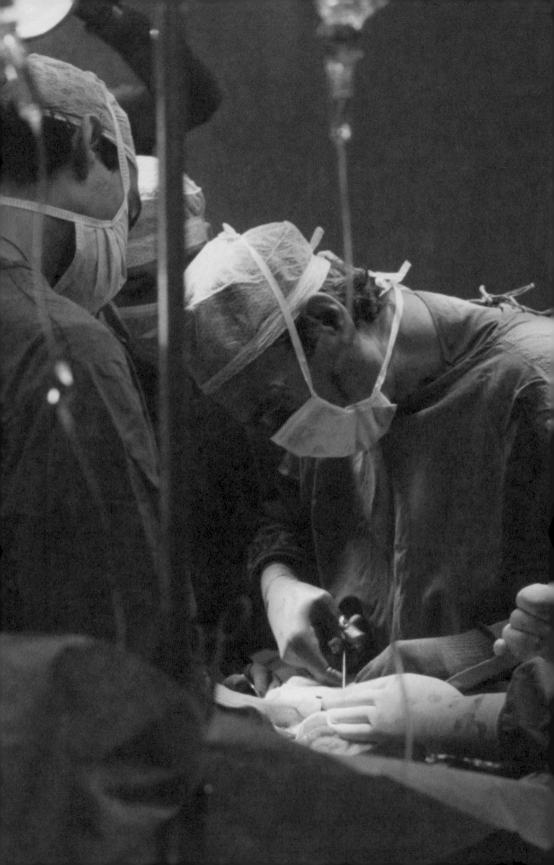

8 TRIALS OF THE BODY

Chapter

❧⟋❀⟍❧

By 1991, Wilma Mankiller could count many great triumphs on the professional level. Behind the scenes, however, she was continuously plagued with physical problems. Back in 1964, while pregnant with her first daughter, Mankiller had suffered a bad kidney infection. Shortly after the death of her father in 1971, these infections began to recur. Tests to discover the problem had not brought good news. Mankiller was stunned to learn that she had the same kidney disease from which her father had died.

The doctors had explained to Mankiller that over time her kidneys would become increasingly diseased until she suffered complete kidney failure. Mankiller had tried to remain optimistic that her kidneys would not completely fail as her father's

A kidney transplant is a two-part operation: one part to remove the healthy kidney from the donor and another part to insert the new kidney into the patient.

had. She tried numerous treatments and surgical procedures. But her condition continued to worsen, and in 1987, shortly before her first election as chief, Mankiller was hospitalized with a long and severe kidney infection. Unfortunately, while in the hospital her condition had been misdiagnosed. This had led to massive kidney damage that could not be reversed. To survive, she would ultimately need a kidney transplant.

In June 1990, well into her first full term as chief, Mankiller underwent the three-hour transplant surgery in Boston. Her eldest brother, Don, who had no trace of the disease, generously acted as her kidney donor.

With a new, well-functioning kidney, Mankiller resumed the duties of her office in August 1990. She continued working as hard as she ever had through the rest of that term and into her next. Her strong vision of a revitalized nation continued to guide her as leader throughout her successful second full term, from 1991 through 1995.

Many people who have suffered kidney damage are kept alive by a process called dialysis. A tube connects a machine to an artery in the patient's arm. Blood flows through the machine, which removes wastes, and then back into the arm. Patients generally undergo dialysis for several hours, three times a week. Other patients have a kidney transplant. The replacement kidney usually comes from a close relative in order for the organ to best match the patient's tissues. But most other replacement organs come from unrelated donors who have died in accidents or from other causes.

But as the 1995 elections loomed, Mankiller began to think deeply about what she wanted for her future. She was torn. Many wanted her to run for chief a third time, and she herself found it hard to imagine not continuing in office. Including her terms as both deputy chief and chief, Mankiller had served the Cherokee Nation a total of 12 years.

And she had done the job with widely acknowledged excellence. Under her leadership, the Cherokee tribe had doubled its membership. By 1991, the nation boasted 108,000 citizens, making it only second in size to the Navajo Nation and the largest nonreservation tribe in the United States. Additionally, the tribal budget had increased to $90 million, nearly twice as large as before Mankiller took office.

Mankiller had presided over the development of an active Job Corps designed to help Cherokee teens acquire the skills they would need for decent employment. Business and industry advancements made during her terms in office were providing

Mankiller's ground-breaking role as first female chief set the stage for many other Native American women to enter into tribal politics. Several have since won political races, both in the Cherokee Nation as well as in other tribes. A few have even been elected chief, or president, of their tribe. One of these is Cecelia Fire Thunder, who took office in December 2004 as the first female leader of the Oglala Sioux, a tribe that has had such famous leaders as Red Cloud and Crazy Horse.

economic aid to many areas of the Cherokee Nation. Under her watch, infant mortality and unemployment were declining, and she had overseen the establishment of cultural programs and health clinics, as well as the important Institute for Cherokee Literacy. The cycle of poverty had been broken for many of her citizens, and deeply ingrained negative stereotypes of Native American people were beginning to dissolve.

During her tenure, Mankiller herself had become a nationally recognized political and spiritual force, as well as a risk-taking social reformer. She had testified before Congress about Indian rights and sovereignty.

Wilma Mankiller and other Native American leaders met with President Bill Clinton to discuss tribal issues.

In 1986, she had been named the American Indian Woman of the Year. The following year, she was named Woman of the Year by the feminist publication *Ms.* magazine. Still, despite her many successes, the work and education yet to be done were limitless.

After giving the matter long thought and discussing the advantages and disadvantages with friends, family, and especially with her husband, Mankiller made the difficult decision. She would not run for chief in 1995. A new phase of her life was about to begin.

Though Mankiller had withdrawn from political life, she was still concerned about many issues, such as minority education and the negative stereotypes of Native Americans. She vowed to continue championing the causes she had focused on in office.

The year 1996 began on a positive note. After stepping down from office, Mankiller accepted a Montgomery Fellowship at Dartmouth College in Hanover, New Hampshire, beginning in January

> *Through the honor of being named* Ms. *magazine's Woman of the Year in 1987, Mankiller became good friends with Gloria Steinem, a famous feminist and the magazine's editor-in-chief. When Steinem got married in 2000, she did so at Mankiller Flats. The ceremony, which was done in part according to Cherokee tradition, was jointly performed by a local judge and Mankiller's husband, Charlie Soap, who is trained in Cherokee spiritual tradition.*

New Hampshire's Dartmouth College was founded in 1769.

1996. She would lecture, take part in seminars, and be able to do much reading, writing, and research in a supportive academic environment.

The only downside of this decision was that Mankiller's husband, Charlie, could not accompany her to the East Coast. Charlie had three sons from former marriages. The two youngest, Cobey and Winterhawk, were still in school in Oklahoma. He needed to stay at home with them.

Without Charlie there, Mankiller was alone and far from Mankiller Flats when pneumonia struck her that winter. She had had colds and other mild physical problems since arriving in Hanover, but expected nothing unusual when she went to be treated for the pneumonia. Instead, she received more distressing news. After all she had been through already, Mankiller had another grave challenge to face. Tests revealed she had lymphoma, a form of cancer.

Devastated by this new attack on her body, Mankiller withdrew from her fellowship in late February, a week before it ended. As she said goodbye to Dartmouth, she did not realize that she would be spending the coming 28 months again battling for her life.

For five weeks in early 1996, Mankiller lay in a Boston hospital. Charlie, other family, and close friends were there to support her, while doctors ran tests and tried to determine the best course of treatment for her. Since her body was already weakened from her kidney transplant, doctors feared traditional cancer treatments might actually prove harmful. So during her long weeks in the hospital, Mankiller explored many different kinds of alternative treatments. She used Native

Cancer is a disease in which cells multiply wildly, destroy healthy tissue, and endanger life. About 100 kinds of cancer attack people. Lymphoma is a cancer of the lymphatic system, a network of vessels that returns fluids to the bloodstream and helps fight disease. It is most often treated through surgery, radiation therapy, or drug therapy (chemotherapy).

American herbal remedies, changed her diet, and practiced meditation.

But in time, it became clear that she needed something stronger. Finally, with her doctors' agreement, Mankiller decided to try a regimen of chemotherapy, which would be followed by radiation treatment.

After completing chemotherapy treatments in August 1996, Mankiller returned home to Oklahoma in the fall to begin radiation. But for all the good these methods did in fighting her cancer, her kidney was now failing rapidly. She began receiving regular dialysis to keep the vital organ functioning, but this led to other problems.

As the determined fighter she had always been, Mankiller braved these assaults on her body. She also remained deeply involved in tribal and community activities. While undergoing treatment, she managed to do fund raising for various important causes, helped her husband build a Boys and Girls Club in Tahlequah, and co-edited a book with her friend Gloria Steinem on American women's history. But her failing health was always at the front of her mind. Throughout 1997, she tried further alternative treatments and endured many blood transfusions. Finally, in early 1998, she was able to declare a significant victory: She had beaten the lymphoma. There was no cancer remaining in her body.

Her kidney, however, continued to fail. Without another transplant operation, Mankiller again faced imminent death. This time, the precious kidney was supplied by Mankiller's niece, 32-year-old Virlee Williamson. The transplant took place in July 1998 and was completely successful. Mankiller's body accepted the new kidney, and it worked properly from the start. Like a cat with nine lives, Mankiller had once again been spared. ✆

While undergoing cancer and kidney treatments, Mankiller spoke at a women's benefit, along with Angela Y. Davis (left) and Gloria Steinem.

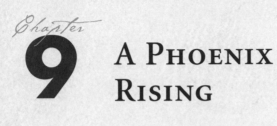

9 A Phoenix Rising

❦

A cat is said to have nine lives. But there is another powerful symbol of rebirth and renewal from the animal kingdom, too. This is the symbol of the phoenix, a legendary bird that rises again from the ashes after being consumed by fire.

This mythical creature is well-known to the Cherokee people. With the push west of the whites in the 1800s, the Cherokee culture nearly went down in flames itself. Today, the Cherokee Nation is again strong and vital, rising from the ashes of a difficult past. This is due in large part to the efforts of Wilma Mankiller.

Mankiller might be considered something of a phoenix, too. She has risen out of adversity time and again, surviving intense challenges, both personal

Wilma Mankiller continues to be active as a speaker, teacher, writer, and activist.

and political. Throughout the most severe physical trials she has prevailed. With another new kidney came new life. And with the turn of the century, Mankiller remains a strong and vibrant leader in Native American issues. She is continually recognized for her invaluable contributions to both Cherokee life and culture, and the world at large.

In 1998, Mankiller was awarded the Presidential Medal of Freedom by President Bill Clinton. This is the highest honor awarded to a civilian by the U.S. government. It recognizes individuals who have made "an especially meritorious contribution to the security or national interests of the United States, or to world peace, or to cultural or other significant public or private endeavors." She has received a Citation for Outstanding Contributions to American Leadership and Native American Culture from the Harvard Foundation (1986). She has also been inducted into the Oklahoma Women's Hall of Fame (1986), Governor's Advisory Committee (1986), and the National Women's Hall of Fame (1993). Mankiller, who was the first in her family

Wilma Mankiller's honors and awards continue to accumulate. But one that stands out as most special to her was a seemingly small gesture. It occurred at a memorial service being presided over by several male tribal elders and clearly indicated the high standing she had achieved among the Cherokees. The men invited her to sit with them in an area designated only for respected elders.

to attend and graduate from college, has also been awarded honorary doctorate degrees from Oklahoma State University, Yale University, and numerous other institutions.

President Bill Clinton awarded Wilma Mankiller with the Presidential Medal of Freedom.

In the spring of 2005, Mankiller was publicly announced as the Morse Chair professor for the fall 2005 semester at the University of Oregon in Eugene. She was selected because of her renown as an activist, her knowledge of legal policy, and her work with Native American tribes. Mankiller accepted the appointment as an opportunity to further causes close to her heart. Topping this list are bringing a broader awareness of contemporary Native American issues, giving such issues a historical context, and casting greater light on Native American stereotypes in order to dissolve them. Her primary duties as professor were public lectures and co-teaching of an ethnic studies class titled "Native American Life, Law, and Leadership" to upper-division students.

Since the time she was a young woman, Mankiller has devoted her life to the service of others. She continues to travel frequently for speaking engagements, to join in panels, and to promote the causes she so deeply believes in. Still, Mankiller finds time to pursue more personal interests as well. She enjoys spending time with family. Her daughters both married men with Cherokee ancestry, and both now have children of their own.

Some of her most enjoyable and relaxing time is spent cooking. She likes to organize groups of women to cook together for tribal events and benefits. In a cookbook she published in 1988, *The Chief Cooks:*

In 1997, Mankiller spoke before a commission about the Cherokee Nation.

Traditional Cherokee Recipes, Mankiller wrote:

> *I appreciate good food and the nurturing it represents. I know also that cooking brings the happiness and warmth synonymous with home and family so important in Cherokee culture.*

Since that time, Mankiller has published other

One of Mankiller's favorite Cherokee recipes is easy to make. Put four cups of chicken broth, four cups of milk, and four cups of water together in a big pot. Add a pound of very finely ground roasted peanuts. Grind about a quarter of the nuts longer than the rest—until you have a thick paste. Add all the nuts to the pot and stir the mixture frequently as it simmers. In about 30 minutes, you've got delicious peanut soup!

books celebrating and educating the public about that which she holds most dear—the cultures of the Cherokee and other indigenous tribes. In 1993, her autobiography, titled *Mankiller: A Chief and Her People*, was released. Her latest book, titled *Every Day Is a Good Day: Reflections of Contemporary Indigenous Women*, was published in 2004.

Mankiller's work and her writings have gone a long way toward establishing respect for Native American culture and building respect for the Cherokee Nation in particular. As she wrote about native cultures in her book *Every Day is a Good Day*, "It is almost impossible for an outsider to grasp the underlying values of the community or the culture and lifeways of the people and their relationship to the natural world."

Like her ancestors who walked the Trail of Tears nearly 170 years ago, Mankiller was torn from that natural world as a child. But the power of the land has remained a major influence in her life. Like those ancestors, she is a survivor. She has survived to pass along greater understanding of her people and their

history to all those who might not have otherwise understood. For this and so many other reasons, Wilma Mankiller will long be known not simply as the first female leader of her nation. She will go down in history as one of the most exceptional and revered of all Cherokee chiefs. ❧

Mankiller's influence on the Cherokee Nation cannot be underestimated.

MANKILLER'S LIFE

1945
Born November 18 in
Tahlequah, Oklahoma

1956
Relocates with
family to
San Francisco,
California

1963
Marries Hector Hugo
Olaya de Bardi in
November

1945

1960

1961
The Berlin Wall is
built, dividing East
and West Germany

1945
World War II
(1939–1945) ends

WORLD EVENTS

1969–1971

Works as an activist during the Native American takeover of Alcatraz Island

1977

Moves back to Mankiller Flats, Oklahoma, and begins working for the Cherokee Nation

1970

1966

The National Organization for Women (NOW) is established to work for equality between women and men

1969

U.S. astronauts are the first humans to land on the moon

1976

U.S. military academies admit women

1979
Suffers a near-fatal automobile accident on November 9

1981
Helps to found the Cherokee Nation Community Development Department

1983
Elected deputy chief of the Cherokee Nation

1980

1978
The first test-tube baby conceived outside its mother's womb is born in Oldham, England

1981
Sandra Day O'Connor becomes the first woman on the U.S. Supreme Court

1983
The AIDS (acquired immune deficiency syndrome) virus is identified

WORLD EVENTS

1985

Succeeds Ross
Swimmer as chief of
the Cherokee Nation

1986

Marries second
husband,
Charlie Soap

1987

Elected first
female chief of the
Cherokee Nation

1985

1985

Associated Press
newsman Terry
Anderson is taken
hostage in Beirut,
Lebanon; he would
be released in
December 1991

1986

The U.S. space shuttle
Challenger explodes,
killing all seven astro-
nauts on board

1987

Stock markets fall
sharply around the
world on Black
Monday, October 19

MANKILLER'S LIFE

1990

Undergoes kidney transplant in June

1991

Elected chief of Cherokee Nation for second term

1995

Retires from public office and accepts a fellowship at Dartmouth University

1990

1990

Political prisoner Nelson Mandela, a leader of the anti-apartheid movement in South Africa, is released; Mandela becomes president of South Africa in 1994

1994

Genocide of 500,000 to 1 million of the minority Tutsi group by rival Hutu people in Rwanda

WORLD EVENTS

1996

Diagnosed with cancer and returns to Mankiller Flats

1998

Defeats cancer but undergoes a second kidney transplant

1999–PRESENT

Continues work as a Native American rights activist and becomes an author, public lecturer, and university professor

1996

A sheep is cloned in Scotland

2005

Major earthquake kills thousands in Pakistan

2001

Terrorist attacks on two World Trade Center Towers in New York City and on the Pentagon in Washington, D.C., leave thousands dead

DATE OF BIRTH: November 18, 1945

BIRTHPLACE: Tahlequah, Oklahoma

FATHER: Charley Mankiller
(1914–1971)

MOTHER: Clara Irene Sitton
Mankiller (1921–)

EDUCATION: Skyline Junior College;
San Francisco State
University; University
of Arkansas

FIRST SPOUSE: Hector Hugo Olaya
de Bardi

DATE OF MARRIAGE: November 13, 1963

CHILDREN: Felicia (1964–)
Gina (1966–)

SECOND SPOUSE: Charlie Lee Soap

DATE OF MARRIAGE: October 1986

FURTHER READING

Kallen, Stuart A. *Native American Chiefs and Warriors*. San Diego, Calif.: Lucent Books, 1999.

Lazo, Caroline Evensen. *Wilma Mankiller*. New York: Dillon Press, 1994.

Schwarz, Melissa. *Wilma Mankiller: Principal Chief of the Cherokees*. New York: Chelsea House, 1994.

Yannuzzi, Della A. *Wilma Mankiller: Leader of the Cherokee Nation*. Hillside, N.J.: Enslow Publishers, 1994.

LOOK FOR MORE SIGNATURE LIVES
BOOKS ABOUT THIS ERA:

Andrew Carnegie: *Captain of Industry*
ISBN 0-7565-0995-5

Carrie Chapman Catt: *A Voice for Women*
ISBN 0-7565-0991

Henry B. Gonzalez: *Congressman of the People*
ISBN 0-7565-0996-3

J. Edgar Hoover: *Controversial FBI Director*
ISBN 0-7565-0997-1

Langston Hughes: *The Voice of Harlem*
ISBN 0-7565-0993-9

Douglas MacArthur: *America's General*
ISBN 0-7565-0994-7

Eleanor Roosevelt: *First Lady of the World*
ISBN 0-7565-0992-0

Franklin Roosevelt: *The New Deal President*
ISBN 0-7565-1586-6

Elizabeth Cady Stanton: *Social Reformer*
ISBN 0-7565-0990-4

Gloria Steinem: *Champion of Womens Rights*
ISBN 0-7565-1587-4

ON THE WEB

For more information on *Wilma Mankiller*, use FactHound.

1. Go to *www.facthound.com*
2. Type in a search word related to this book or this book ID: 0756516005
3. Click on the *Fetch It* button.

FactHound will fetch the best Web sites for you.

HISTORIC SITES

Cherokee Heritage Center
21192 Keeler
Park Hill, OK 74451
918/456-6007
Two reconstructed Cherokee villages, a Trail of Tears exhibit, art galleries, and a 4,000-volume library

New Echota—First Capital of the Cherokee Nation
1211 Chatsworth Highway N.E.
Calhoun, GA 30701
706/624-1321
Historic town containing the Cherokee Supreme Court building, historic Cherokee homes, and a museum of Cherokee history

arson
setting a fire for the purpose of doing harm

bureaucratic
a way of doing things characterized by time-consuming effort and complications

chemotherapy
the use of drugs or chemicals to combat disease

clan
a group of people related by a common ancestor

dialysis
a process that uses a machine to remove waste from the blood, a process usually performed by the human kidneys

evicted
forced out

facilitator
one who helps something to happen

feminist
someone who believes strongly that women ought to have the same opportunities and rights as men have

foreboding
a feeling that something bad is about to occur

grassroots
dealing at the most fundamental, person-to-person level

homestead
to acquire and settle on a piece of land

idyllic
picturesque, simple, and natural

indigenous
originating in a particular environment or geographical region

inducted
admitted as a member

literacy
the ability to read and write

mandate
authorization for a leader to take command due to
widespread public favor

muscular dystrophy
a chronic disease of the muscles that causes varying degrees
of weakness in the voluntary muscles of the body

shaman
a religious leader and healer of a tribe

syllabary
a series or set of written characters in which each character
is used to represent a syllable

tenure
term in office

Chapter 1

Page 10, line 5: Wilma Mankiller and Michael Wallis. *Mankiller: A Chief and Her People.* New York: St. Martin's Press, 1993, p. 14.

Chapter 2

Page 23, line 12: Ibid., p 32.

Page 26, sidebar: Ibid., p. 77.

Chapter 3

Page 37, sidebar: Ibid., p. 83.

Chapter 4

Page 43, line 14: Ibid., p. 159.

Chapter 5

Page 52, line 14: Ibid., p. 205.

Chapter 6

Page 62, line 2: Ibid., pp. 223–224.

Page 63, sidebar: Ibid., p. 226.

Chapter 7

Page 73, line 8: Ibid., p. 247.

Page 77, sidebar: Wilma Mankiller. "Rebuilding the Cherokee Nation." Sweet Briar College. April 2, 1993. *Gifts of Speech.* 30 Nov. 2005. http://gos.sbc.edu/m/mankiller.html

Chapter 9

Page 90, line 12: *Code of Federal Regulations.* Title 32, Section 578.4.

Page 93, line 2: Beverly Cox and Martin Jacobs. "Mankiller Cooking: The Chief Chef." *Native Peoples.* Sept./Oct. 2003, p. 22.

Page 94, line 19: Wilma Mankiller. *Every Day Is a Good Day: Reflections of Contemporary Indigenous Women.* Golden, Colo.: Fulcrum Publishing, 2004, p. 30.

Adcock, Clifton. "Mankiller Helped Lead the Way in Oklahoma." *Muskogee Daily Phoenix and Times-Democrat* (OK). November 27, 2004.

"Alcatraz is Not an Island." Indian Activism/PBS Web site. <http://www.pbs. org/itvs/alcatrazisnotanisland/activism.html> 12 April 2005.

Carter III, Samuel. *Cherokee Sunset: A Nation Betrayed.* Garden City, N.Y.: Doubleday & Co., Inc., 1976.

Cox, Beverly, and Martin Jacobs. "Mankiller Cooking: The Chief Chef." *Native Peoples.* Sept./Oct. 2003.

Ehle, John. *Trail of Tears: The Rise and Fall of the Cherokee Nation.* New York: Doubleday, 1988.

Fischer, Kent. "Lessons in Tolerance: Former Cherokee Chief Brings Experience to Dartmouth." *Black Issues in Higher Education.* Jan. 25, 1996.

Gilbert, Joan. *The Trail of Tears Across Missouri.* Columbia: University of Missouri Press, 1996.

Kilpatrick, Alan. *The Night Has a Naked Soul: Witchcraft and Sorcery Among the Western Cherokee.* Syracuse, N.Y.: Syracuse University Press, 1998.

Mankiller, Wilma. "Education and Native Americans: Entering the Twenty-First Century on Our Own Terms." *National Forum.* Spring, 1991.

Mankiller, Wilma. *Every Day Is a Good Day: Reflections of Contemporary Indigenous Women.* Golden, Colo.: Fulcrum Publishing, 2004.

Mankiller, Wilma, and Michael Wallis. *Mankiller: A Chief and Her People.* New York: St. Martin's Griffin, 1993.

Mankiller, Wilma. "People Expect Me to be More Warlike." *U.S. News & World Report.* Feb. 17, 1986.

Waldman, Carl. *Atlas of the North American Indian.* New York: Checkmark Books, 2000.

Waldrop, Judith. "Mankiller's Challenge." *American Demographics.* June 1987.

Woster, Terry. "More Women Buck Tradition, Take Reins of Indian Tribes." *Muskogee Daily Phoenix and Times-Democrat* (OK). November 27, 2004.

About the Author

Pamela Dell began her professional career writing for adults and started writing for children about 12 years ago. Since then she has published fiction and nonfiction books, written numerous magazine articles, and created award-winning interactive multimedia.

Image Credits

Marcy Nighswander/AP Wide World Photos, cover (top), 4–5, 76, 82, 100 (top left); Courtesy of Felicia Olaya, cover (bottom), 2, 88, 101 (top); Woolaroc Museum, Bartlesville, Oklahoma, 8; The Granger Collection, New York, 11; Nancy Carter/North Wind Picture Archives, 14; John Elk III, 16, 21, 35; Western History Collections, University of Oklahoma Library, 19; Kevin Fleming/Corbis, 22; North Wind Picture Archives, 25, 31; Charles E. Rotkin/Corbis, 28, 96 (top); San Francisco History Center, San Francisco Public Library, 33, 36; Bettmann/Corbis, 38, 45, 47, 67, 68, 97 (top left); Ted Streshinsky/Corbis, 41; Ernst Haas/Getty Images, 42; Dorothy Tidwell Sullivan, 48, 60; Bob Rowan/Progressive Image/Corbis, 51; Marilyn "Angel" Wynn, 54, 62, 65, 71 (bottom), 75, 97 (top right), 98; Steve Liss/Time Life Pictures/Getty Images, 57; Courtesy Wilma Mankiller, 58; Robert Dechert Collection, Annenberg Rare Book and Manuscript Library, University of Pennsylvania, 71 (top); AP Wide World Photos, 72, 99 (top); Vittoriano Rastelli/Corbis, 78; Yogi, Inc./Corbis, 84, 100 (top right); Don West/AP Wide World Photos, 87; Paul J. Richards/AFP/Getty Images, 91; *Tulsa World*, Tom Gilbert/AP Wide World Photos, 93; Peter Turnley/Corbis, 95; Library of Congress, 96 (bottom), 97 (bottom left); NASA, 97 (bottom right), 99 (bottom); Scott Peterson/Liaison/Getty Images, 100 (bottom); Getty Images, 101 (bottom left); Farooq Naeem/AFP/Getty Images, 101 (bottom left).